KiD YOUTUBER PRESENTS:

HALL MONITORS

TOTAL ECLIPSE OF THE ART

By Marcus Emerson

This one's for the Lacey's...

Emerson Publishing House

Book design by Marcus Emerson
Art created digitally in Clip Studio Pro.

Not that I get paid or anything. That's just something people say when their job starts to feel like the same ol' grind every day, I guess.

I mean, being a Hall Monitor is totally my favorite part of me, but sometimes it can get a little repetitive, you know what I mean? Especially when dealing with some of the students at Wood Intermediate.

They're forever trying to find new and creative ways to break the rules, but no matter how inventive they are with whatever party they're poppin' – it all leads to the same place...

And today was no different.

Me and Vayla were responding to a 10-13 – safety hazard – in the main hall. Apparently, some student had taped several plastic sheets together and laid them across the length of the entire hallway.

I didn't know exactly what the sheets were for, but I had a hunch. And if that hunch was correct, then that meant we needed to hurry up before it was too late...

A "safety hazard" didn't really describe what we were heading towards, but it was the closest thing we had in our Hall Monitor 10 Codes book, which was surprising because I'd spent HOURS thinking up every possible emergency code I could think of...

I ran full speed, my feet pounding on the floor, until I finally saw the end of the plastic sheets along with the kid who was responsible for the 10-13.

The kid who's been a splinter in my eye since the first day of school. The kid who thinks he's all that, and a bag of chips. The kid tryin' to hit the big-time by filming INCREDIBLY irresponsible stunts AT SCHOOL for his YouTube channel.

That kid was Davy Spencer, AKA, Kid Youtuber, and apparently, the stunt on today's menu was a...

Obviously, that waterslide was a big ol' honkin' NOPE with a side of NUH-UH, and an extra side of NOT ON MY WATCH, not only because it was a TRIP hazard, but it was also a SLIP hazard! I mean, c'mon! Water in the hallways?? Was he nuts??

So, I did what I had to and shut the whole thing down. Or at least, I TRIED to. On a another note, I think the tread on my shoes might be a little worn down...

It's been about a minute since the last season of Hall Monitors, and I'd love to tell you that we've been busting bad guys left and right, but to be honest, things have been pretty quiet since then.

I mean, it's not like NOTHING has happened. There's always plenty of work for me and the other monitors to keep us busy every day, but it's just little things – side quests and stuff, y'know?

Like when the school ran out of hall passes and me and Vayla Patel were given a bunch of escort quests for kids who needed to use the bathroom during class...

Escort quests are fine and all, but they CAN BE kind of annoying since they have a tendency to spawn additional quests as well...

Chad Schulte's been hard at work starting a mobile unit for the Hall Monitor program. He spent DAYS back at HQ fixing up a super rad scooter to ride in the hallways. After he was done, I gotta admit - that thing was the sickest ride this side of the gymnasium.

And EVERYBODY thought it was cool.

Everybody except the ONE PERSON who needed to...

●REC

Scooters are great, but not INSIDE a school.

PRINCIPAL HAWKINS

Obviously, that was a bummer, not only for Chad but for the whole squad. So while we still have a mobile unit, it's just not one we're allowed to use...

I thought Hawkins said you couldn't ride that.

He said I couldn't RIDE it. He never said I couldn't STAND next to it.

Anyways, that brings us to Charlotte Lovejoy and Victor Espinoza. Those two have been tag-teaming a giant sign for a thing that was coming up for the school.

Those two vibe hard together when it comes to monitoring the halls, but when it comes to carpentry, they butt heads more than two goats in a head-butting contest...

Anyways, you're probably wondering why those two were even building a sign instead of doing Hall Monitor stuff, aren't you?

Well, it's cool. As the Hall Monitor Captain, I let 'em do it since we didn't have much to do at the moment. It's not like we were busy with a big-time case or anything, so I figured they could be helpful somewhere else.

I mean, the truth is – I WISH we were busy with a big-time case, especially after LAST season. After I got that sweet taste of victory from solving a mystery, that's all I crave now!

I want it so bad that it's gotten to the point where I'm desperately searching for it, even in the dumbest places...

But big-time cases just aren't part of the everyday life of a Hall Monitor. Forgotten locker combinations, lost phones, catching chickens in the school – that's the kinds of things WE take care of.

And those things are important, but c'mon, how cool would it be if a big-time case rolled up on us?

Anyways, it was Wednesday afternoon, just before lunch, and I was on my normal patrol through the school, making sure things were cool.

Lunch can get a little cray around here, but does that surprise anyone? That's just what happens when kids are stuck in classrooms for hours without bail.

All the hangry and pent-up energy becomes unshackled at the same time by every single student, all burning with the same simplistic need – food.

Sometimes it's fine.

But sometimes this place turns into that one scene from the Lion King when all those deer-looking things came wildly running down the hill...

Today's lunch was a little different, though. There was a lot more energy than usual in the cafeteria, but not a chaotic kind of energy. It was more like a buzz of excitement in the air.

A bunch of students were onstage, setting up for a 6th grade art show that was gonna be held on Friday. BTW – that's what the sign is for that Espinoza and Lovejoy were working on.

Anyways, the guy in charge of the show was Mr. Reynolds...

FYI – Mr. Reynolds isn't a teacher at Wood. He's a substitute art teacher who's subbing for Ms. Bane, who's taking a week-long vacation at the happiest place on Earth, which is kinda funny because if you knew Ms. Bane, then you'd know that she's not exactly the happiest person on Earth.

I don't think I've ever seen that woman smile, not even once. Principal Hawkins even asked her to send a pic of herself on one of the rollercoasters to put in the yearbook, and she's not even smiling on THAT thing.

I mean, how can you NOT smile on a rollercoaster??

So anyways, Mr. Reynolds is in while she's out for the week, which is pretty sweet because he's kinda become famous for putting on snaz-a-delic art shows.

Everybody's forever talking about how EXCITING they are, but I don't know – staring at paintings? That doesn't SOUND exciting, but maybe that's just me.

Well, actually they might be talking about the fact that his art shows are also CONTESTS. Students get to vote on which art is the best art, and the winner gets an ArtPad Pro – a 13-inch digital drawing pad that costs two thousand smackeroos.

Mr. Reynolds was using a token system for votes. Every student at Wood got one token – a gold-colored plastic coin – to cast a vote with by dropping it into a little box next to the artwork they liked the most. The one with the most tokens would win the ArtPad Pro.

So I guess THAT'S kind of exciting.

Word on the playground was that the ArtPad Pro was paid for by Mr. Reynolds himself. Apparently, being a substitute teacher is where you make the big bucks...

The show didn't start until 8th period, and then it was gonna stay up until the end of the school day on Friday, when the winner got announced.

Kids were supposed to bring their art to the stage during lunch, but not all of them did. I'd say outta the 44 entered into the show, about half of them showed up with their paintings or sculptures. The rest either forgot or were frantically trying to finish their pieces before 8th period.

Anyways, as the other Hall Monitors kept their eyes on the cafeteria, I decided to take a stroll through the art that HAD been set up.

I'm not an art critic, but I had to admit that a lot of the artwork was actually kinda cool. Like the oil painting that Fergus Widdershim had made of Dutch McKenzie wearing a suit and looking deep in thought.

And Josh Lucey's ink drawing of a... well, I actually didn't know what the heck it was...

Then there was artwork that was kinda "meh," like Emma Walsh's painting of a flamingo...

But then there was a piece of art that LITERALLY didn't belong up there. Something that had obviously been thrown together and entered into the show as a last second addition instead of getting thrown into the trash where it belonged!

I couldn't believe Mr. Reynolds let Davy into the show! Davy put, like, ZERO effort into that dumb spud!

I mean, it was obvious that he just grabbed a baked potato from one of the lunch ladies, drew a face on it with a paint marker, stabbed it with toothpicks, and was now calling it art.

I bet you Davy was only in the show because he'd just found out about the ArtPad Pro and wanted a shot at winning it!

So by the end of lunch, the exhibit was only half-full with empty slots sprinkled throughout, and art pinned to temporary pop-up walls and sitting on tables.

And even though several kids hadn't posted their work yet, only one missing artist stuck out – Annie Yun.

ICYDK, Annie is the best artist at our school, maybe even the city – I wouldn't be surprised if it was actually the whole country. That's why we all wanted to see what she had created.

Not only is Annie GOOD at art, she's SMART at art, too. Like, her art always has a message. Usually it's a message that goes over everyone's head, but that's only because she might be a legit genius.

I mean, for real, the fact that her art was late to the show WASN'T an accident. It was ON PURPOSE because she WANTED to leave us in suspense...

Mr. Reynolds might as well send that ArtPad Pro home with Annie because as long as she's in the show, nobody else even has a chance at winning that thing.

Every class in the school got to skip part of their 8th period class to go down to the cafeteria and check out all the cool drawings and paintings and sculptures the 6th graders had worked so hard on.

There was still a ton of artwork that hadn't gotten turned in, which meant there were still empty spaces in the show. Mr. Reynolds wasn't worried about it, though. He just shrugged it off, and said...

But the painting that everybody WANTED to see had finally arrived. At the start of 8th period, Annie brought her painting out from hiding, and unveiled it for the world to see.

And I gotta be honest – something inside of me changed. Until that moment, I'd thought art was just something cool to look at. I never thought that a painting would ever get me right in the feels, but somehow hers did.

It was glorious.

Unexpected.

Entertaining.

It was Davy Spencer.

Davy wasn't too happy when he found out about the painting, obvi. He even tried to get Mr. Reynolds to take it down because he said he never gave Annie permission to use his face, but Mr. Reynolds just said she didn't need his permission since her art was considered a parody...

Voting for the winner had officially begun, and students had until the end of the day Friday to cast their vote.

Not all of them wanted to wait, though.

Little boxes next to paintings started clinking with tokens getting dropped inside. Some boxes had one or two tokens. Some had more. Some had none. Davy's had more than a few, which surprised me, but not Vayla.

Some of the other artists weren't too happy about that, no surprise there. I mean, just LOOK at this thing...

And even though Davy had a bunch of tokens in his box, it was nothing compared to Annie's. She was already taking the lead, and the show still had two days to go!

Hey, Davy Spencer might actually have a shot at winning the show after all – just not how he thought!

But FYI – we weren't dealing with REAL tattoos. No, REAL tattoos would most definitely be a problem too big for the Hall Monitors to handle. What we were dealing with was a bunch of kids going into the boy's locker room and paying a couple bucks to get their arms drawn on with a Sharpie marker.

Was that against the rules? You can bet your freakin' life it is. That's a straight-up 10-34 – illegal tattoo parlor on school grounds! Duh!

Fresh tats like that leave ink on whatever they touch! So desks and walls and water fountains all over the school were getting covered with black doodle marks. The whole school was starting to look like a page outta one of my sketchbooks!

Me and Chad got to the boy's locker room lickety-split and found the place jammin' with students waiting to get inked. Me and Chad followed the line of kids into the dark and skeevy locker room as fluorescent lights buzzed and flickered overhead.

Some of the kids glared at us as we passed them. Others avoided eye contact completely.

And to be honest, I was scared. Like SCARED, scared. I mean, it was my first time dealing with a 10-34, so I didn't know what to expect!

But onward we delved, all the way to the unused showers in the back – that's where I heard the artist talking to his client about what to draw on her arm.

I stopped. Waited outside the shower to collect myself. Then, after some calming breath exercises, I jumped around the corner to face my fears.

Turns out... I had nothing to be scared of at all.

The next morning, I got to school around seven in the a.m. nice and early. I like to walk the halls before students arrive just to make sure the place is tidied up before classes start.

I mean, I don't CLEAN the school or anything, but I like to do the stuff the janitors don't get paid to do, like straightening posters in the hallways...

Or sweeping the leaves off the sidewalk outside...

But sometimes I like to get there early to hang out in the teacher's lounge and catch up on episodes of my newest obsession – The Great Caveman Bake Off...

But I can only watch people bake goodies for so long before needing one for myself, so I punched the Pause button and ran down to the cafeteria to hit up one of the vending machines.

Usually, the lunchroom is empty that early in the morning, so I was a bit surprised when Emma Walsh walked out just as I walked in...

I ran over to the vending machines, fed my dollar bill into one of the slots, and dialed in the number for chocolate cupcakes.

My snack fell to the bottom of the machine, but before I could grab it, a sound came from the stage that totally freaked me out...

With my heart racing, I dashed over to the stage, worried that one of the pop-up walls with artwork had fallen over or something, but they were all still standing.

I climbed the stairs and slowly scanned the art show, looking for any signs of damage, and that's when I noticed a small trail of water slowly seeping out from the bottom of one of the walls.

I suddenly heard the sound of squeaking sneakers suddenly racing across the empty cafeteria floor. I knew the sound of guilty footsteps when I heard 'em.

But when I turned to look, they were already gone, the cafeteria door slowly shutting behind them.

In a stroke of luck, the door immediately pulled open and in walked Davy Spencer.

I stood onstage, dumbfounded, thankful I wasn't in the middle of a play with a thousand kids watching me.

The water on the floor had reached my shoes. Slowly, with little squeaks of my own, I followed it across the stage until I found where it was coming from.

My blood went ice-cold as my stomach sunk.

One student's artwork had been completely drenched, blue and red paint bleeding down the canvas and turning purple on the floor.

The only reason I knew who it belonged to was because it was the best painting I'd ever set my eyes on.

It was Annie's.

And now it was ruined.

I couldn't believe that a student at my school would stoop so low to destroy something someone had worked their buns off on, but I guess that's the way the cookie crumbles sometimes.

The kid who sabotaged Annie's painting – henceforth to be referred to as the Vandal – was still out there, and I needed him to know that he hadn't gotten away with it, so I ran to the front office as soon as homeroom started and made an announcement over the P.A.

Me and the other monitors taped off the crime scene to keep people from tampering with the evidence, but since we STILL didn't have any official police tape, I asked Lovejoy if she could whip up something similar...

Vayla went to Annie's homeroom class to get her so she could identify the canvas, but Annie wasn't there.

Instead, Vayla found her at Davy Spencer's locker, grabbing stuff for class or something...

Sharing lockers probably wasn't the most hygienic thing to do, but it wasn't against the rules, so whatevs.

Anyways, Vayla brought Annie down to the lunchroom where she confirmed that the rekt canvas was, in fact, her own.

But the weird thing was that she didn't seem to even care about it. She didn't freak out or cry or even get angry.

All she said was...

I even tried offering some words of encouragement, telling her that Mr. Reynolds would probably give her a redo, but she just wasn't into it.

I guess that's a normal response when someone's in shock, but Annie wasn't that either.

I mean, she just shrugged a shoulder and then skipped off like it was no big deal...

Oh well. Annie might not have cared, but I did.

And in case you're wondering, Davy WASN'T the Vandal. Honestly, I really wished he was cuz that would've made my job SO much easier, but I checked his shoes.

The Vandal's were wet; Davy's were bone dry.

He was only in the cafeteria to check on his potato because he was worried that it was in danger.

Mr. Reynolds tried sending me off to class after him and Principal Hawkins showed up. Said they'd handle it from there, but there was no way I was about to leave the cafeteria, not after the atrocities that'd been committed!

What the what was wrong with that guy??

Didn't he understand??

There was a criminal on the loose!

Suspects to find!

Motives to uncover!

In fact, I was starting to think the whole show needed to be put on pause. I mean, if the city was donating money for the ArtPad Pro, then they'd probably wanna be notified, too!

We needed to take this directly to the mayor himself!

Mr. Reynolds thought that wasn't such a great idea since the mayor probably had more important things to worry about, but what could be more important than the untimely death of Annie's painting?

Then, to my surprise, Principal Hawkins took my side.

He said I was allowed to investigate as long as it wasn't disruptive and didn't interfere with any other activities in the school, which was totes cool with me.

Me and Hawkins have had our differences in the past, but he was finally starting to respect my authority...

And that was that - the Case of the Sabotaged Painting had officially kicked off...

Mr. Reynolds grabbed a mop and started cleaning up the mess onstage. Hawkins peaced out along with the rest of my monitors, except for Vayla.

She tags along on pretty much ALL my patrols, but it's cool. We've sorta got this mentor/apprentice thing going on between us...

Anyways, Annie's painting was DRONCHED. The canvas was practically washed clean. The puddle under it was now a thick sludge of purple color that Mr. Reynolds was slowly sopping up.

I took a knee.

Ran two fingers through the mush of paint-water.

Wasn't thick.

Wasn't thin either.

Then I brought my fingers up and studied the purple paste. To the naked eye it would appear to be watered-down paint, nothing more. But to my trained detective's eye, there was a whole world of evidence waiting to be found, namely the itty-bitty slivers of latex playing hide 'n seek in the ooze...

The "how" was figured out, so now the million-dollar question was "why?"

WHY would somebody ruin Annie's painting?

Ding, ding ding! Vayla was right!

Annie was easily gonna score first place in the show. I mean, it was no-contest contest. The box by her ruined art was already half-filled with tokens.

If she was forced out, then SOMEONE ELSE would have a chance at winning the ArtPad Pro for themselves, which meant EVERYBODY in the show was now a suspect.

But with that many suspects, who was I even supposed to investigate first??

That's when I suddenly remembered...

For the record, I doubted that Emma was the Vandal since she was in the cafeteria BEFORE the water balloon had popped.

Besides Davy, she was the only other person in there that morning, so it only made sense to question her first.

But now that EVERYBODY in the show was a suspect, I also needed the names of all the students who had artwork on that stage, which Mr. Reynolds was cool with getting for me.

But "later" wasn't good enough for me!

"Later" just gave the Vandal time to make their escape to the Galápagos Islands where they'd spend the rest of their life riding sea lions off into sunsets, and I know that doesn't make any sense, but I'm stressed, and I can't think straight when I'm stressed!

So I was about to straight-up ask Mr. Reynolds if we could go find the list right now, but that's when something caught my eye on the cafeteria floor.

Faded footprints that led away from Annie's painting.

It was a CLUE!

I jumped down to check out the footprints, which had all dried out by then. The only reason they were still visible was because they were a slight shade of purple – the same shade of purple that Mr. Reynolds was mopping up. Vayla snapped a picture of the footprint and continued to study it on her phone...

Reebuks are famous for their star logo, which is under the heel on every pair of Reebuks ever made.

And Vayla was right – the star on the Vandal's footprints were practically gone, almost completely worn off.

That was HUGE.

That meant all we had to do was find the student in the art show who had a pair of Reebuks with worn off stars on the heels.

But first... we had to get to class.

So, uh, an anonymous student tipped us off about some weird sounds they heard in the library, soooo... follow me, I guess.

It was like Lovejoy said – a student-who-shall-not-be-named gave us a tip about some strange scratching sounds coming from underneath the study desks in the library.

What we were dealing with was very probably a shaky air vent or something. Maybe a wobbly table leg scraping against the tables, I don't know.

As soon as Lovejoy got to the library, she went over to the study desks and confirmed that there were, in fact, scratching sounds coming from under there.

She got on the ground, turned on her phone flashlight, and bravely shined it in the darkness...

And that's when Lovejoy spotted it – the LIVING source of the scratching sounds...

Lucky for us the whole thing turned out to be a false alarm, and the scratching sounds were coming from a cutey patootie puppy that had snuck into the school.

I spent most of the morning stressing about all the "What ifs?" What if I failed to find the Vandal? What if the other Hall Monitors quit because I couldn't solve the case? What if Hawkins replaced me because I failed? What if goblins were real? What if they started a war with humans? Would I be too young to fight? I mean, I'd WANNA fight, but 11 years old might be too young to join the war...

But as heavy as those questions were, I knew I had to shake them off. They were the kind of questions that only come from fear, and that kind of fear is a liar.

I was GOING to solve the case.

Even if I needed a little bit of help doing it.

Which was why I was waiting for SkullCap at his designated meeting spot.

FYI - Skullcap is some mystery kid running around in a mask and cape. Not sure if he's a good guy or a bad guy, but my heart tells me I can trust him.

My heart also tells me I can trust dairy, but my gut is pretty against that, so... yeah, whatever.

I hadn't seen Skullcap since last season, but a while ago he'd left a package back at HQ with a small helium tank, some balloons, and instructions on how to get ahold of him if necessary...

So I went upstairs, waited and waited and waited, and then felt pretty dumb about the whole thing after the bell rang and Skullcap was a no-show.

Ugh.

See if I ever do THAT again.

Discouraged, I walked over to the mirror to look myself in the eye and wonder what the heck I was even doing with my life, and that's when I suddenly saw Skullcap standing behind me in the reflection...

I gotta admit, THAT was good. Not sure how he snuck into the bathroom without me noticing, though.

I mean, the only way he could've done that was by already hiding out in one of the stalls and waiting until the bell rang to make his ninja-like appearance...

That's exactly what I did.

SKULLCAP

There were a million other questions I had about the logistics of his sudden appearance, but I had a case to solve, so I just dove right in, showing him the pics of the footprints with the missing stars on the heels that Vayla had texted me. He studied them quietly for a moment, chewing his lip. Then he said...

Okay, OBVIOUSLY we weren't dealing with a vampire, but my brain was playing the "What if?" game again.

Skullcap stared at the footprint on my phone for another couple seconds. I wasn't sure if he was gonna have anything useful to add, but he surprised me...

Of course! This school has so many clubs that it wouldn't surprise me if there was one for walking, and since I still had to find Emma, I was happy to let Skullcap look into it for me.

And because I was gonna talk to Emma, I checked my hair in the mirror real quick to make sure my curls were curlin' because I... um... I think Emma's kinda... uh... I mean, whatever, you get what I'm trying to say.

Then I turned back to thank Skullcap, but he was already gone...

During my meeting with Skullcap, Vayla had been patiently waiting outside the bathroom for me. We were gonna try and find Emma during the break, but since my talk with Skullcap went a little long, we were just gonna have to find her during her fourth period class – gym, which would've been super easy to do if it weren't for the fact that her whole class was outside playing pickleball by the time we got there.

ICYDK, pickleball is a game where you hit a plastic ball back and forth over a net, which is something I wish someone had told me before the first time I tried playing it with the other monitors for one of our team-building exercises...

Anyways, Emma's class was in an empty part of the parking lot, playing the game with portable nets.

Me and Vayla looked all over the place for the gym teacher – Miss Gymalski, the Olympic weightlifter from Austria – to ask if we could borrow Emma for a few minutes, but we couldn't find her anywhere.

Josh Lucey was easy to find, though – the kid with the octophant drawing in the show. It's just too bad we weren't looking for HIM...

Crack the case yet, Sherlock?

Not yet, Josh.

There were, like, eight pickleball games going on, and one of them must've been a big deal because there was a whole crowd of kids huddled around it.

I figured Gymalski was probably at the game with the crowd, reffing or something, so me and Vayla headed that way.

But when we got closer, I discovered that Miss Gymalski wasn't reffing the game at all.

She was actually PLAYING in it.

Not only that, but she was playing against the very person we'd come to see – Emma Walsh.

Well, PLAYING wasn't exactly the right word.

I think the more accurate word was LOSING...

I tried getting Gymalski's attention, but she couldn't hear me over all the kids shouting and making bets on who was gonna win the match.

Gambling is a big no-no at Wood, but with the amounts of cash being put on the lines, I kinda doubted that anybody was serious about the action.

I waved my arms at Gymalski while Vayla tried getting Emma to even LOOK at her, but the game was heated, and both Gymalski and Emma were in the zone.

Emma was ahead by one, so all she needed was one more point to beat the gym teacher and become a legend at the school.

I gotta admit, "The Girl Who Beat the Olympian" has a nice ring to it.

Emma's moment had come.

Up until now, she'd been playing a game of pickleball like a normal human being, but something in her had just changed...

Her hunger for victory burned deep in her eyes.

I saw it.

Vayla saw it.

Her classmates saw it.

Even Miss Gymalski saw it.

And it made her shudder.

But just before Emma could serve the ball, Miss Gymalski suddenly spotted me and Vayla standing off to the side...

I don't know. The timing of Gymalski noticing us seemed a little shady. And I only say that because she didn't PAUSE the game between her and Emma. She ENDED it...

Ah-ha! Emma exit court and forfeit! I am winner winner chicken dinner!!

Emma was pretty upset that we messed up her game, no surprise there, but she was still cooperative.

As she walked over, I glanced at her shoes to check if they were Reebuks – just to make sure she wasn't the one with the squeaky shoes in the cafeteria.

They weren't – they were Old Balances – so I went ahead and proceeded with the questioning, which actually didn't take as long as I thought it would...

Like, literally, 10 seconds.

Okay, I'll admit that I'm not the world's best detective, but I'm working on it! I mean, yeah, I was about to walk away defeated, but only because I didn't really know what else to ask.

Lucky for me, Vayla was there to help with that...

Oh, man, that little bit of information was WAY huger than Emma realized. I mean, she might've just solved the case without even knowing it!

There was only ONE girl at Wood named Hazel, and the only reason I know that was because her last name is Basil, so whenever you say her full name, it always sounds like you're calling her by an adorable nickname.

But just like most kids with adorable nicknames, she HATES it.

Even when it's teachers taking attendance...

Emma was innocent, that much was obvious.

I mean, she wasn't even in the cafeteria when Annie's painting got splashed, so she was pretty much off the hook just because of that.

But I didn't wanna just bail and be like, "See ya later!" since we kinda ruined the pickleball game between her and Miss Gymalski.

I still felt bad about that, so me and Vayla spent the rest of fourth period playing doubles against the two of them.

And I gotta say – pickleball is kind of a fun game.

Especially when your opponents spend all their time talking smack to each other.

Look, I like videogames as much as the next guy, but there's a time and a place for them, and during school hours is NOT the time OR the place.

And I know that some schools use videogames as rewards or even as teaching tools, like the forever popular Oregon Trail where you take your family across the country and hope that none of your children die of starvation and then you gotta leave them – the foundation of your unconditional, undying love – buried in some random field that a fast food joint will probably build their restaurant on top of 150 years later...

Yeah, I'm not talkin' about that. I'm talkin' about Mario Kart. Yeah, some kid brought Mario Kart.

It didn't take me long to find the tournament after I got to the library, so I went in ready to shut the whole thing down. But before I could say anything, the kid with the Switch goes...

What can I say? I was weak.

During lunch, I was on my own. Vayla went on patrol with Chad while Espinoza and Lovejoy went to work on their art show sign, which was coming along pretty nicely, except for a minor spelling error. The sign was supposed to say "Winner" at the top, but instead...

I needed to find Hazel in the lunchroom, but before that, I went over to the art room to see if Mr. Reynolds had found the list of all the kids in the art show yet, but apparently, he'd forgotten about it.

No big deal. It was only the middle of the school day. I'd circle back and get the list from him later.

The lunchroom was the usual swirl of activity. Kids walking aisles with trays of food, sitting at tables with friends, or just standing around and hanging out.

As I searched for Hazel in the sea of students, all I heard were kids talking about who might've sabotaged Annie's painting, which wasn't a surprise since her ruined canvas was still on display onstage facing the room, almost like the smudged-up painting was the art itself.

A cluster of students stood at the foot of the stage curiously studying the damage that'd been done.

I walked the aisles, looking for Hazel in the mess of hungry students until I finally found her at a table with her friends. She was holding a half-eaten PB&J sammy... and her hands?

They were a light shade of purple, just like Emma had said.

All I needed to do was walk up to her cool, calm, and collected-like and ask why her hands were purple, no big deal. Pretty easy, right?

Too bad I botched it by getting overly excited instead...

Hazel slid off her seat and took off like a freakin' gazelle. I tried going after her, but it wasn't easy with all the kids blocking my way.

At the end of the aisle, Hazel took a sharp turn and beelined toward the stage.

If I didn't act fast, she was gonna get away!

I climbed on top of one of the tables and hopped from one to the other until I was ahead of her. I thought she was gonna try to escape out of one of the doors behind the stage, so I needed to get up there in order to cut her off.

I skidded to a stop, planted my feet, and – I do not know why I did this – I launched myself into the air like I was gonna fly across the room like Superman.

Obviously, that didn't work, but man, I WISH I could fly.

I landed hard on the stage and rolled across it until I bumped into Davy's pedestal – the one with the ugly spud – knocking the potato right off.

I rolled over, embarrassed, staring at the ceiling.

Hazel had gotten away, probably already on the phone with Uber to come pick her up to drive her to the Galápagos Islands. I had lost my shot at catching the Vandal. I had fumbled the whole thing.

Or at least, I THOUGHT I had fumbled the whole thing.

As I stared at the ceiling, Hazel's face slowly came into view as she hovered over me...

Those weren't exactly the actions of a GUILTY kid. I turned my head to get a look at her shoes, hoping they were the Reebuks with the missing stars.

But they weren't. They were Skreechers.

She helped me up and we found an empty table. Without the Reebuks, all I had were her purple hands, so I asked about them.

From where we were sitting, I could see her painting on one of the pop-up walls on the stage.

Yup. Definitely purple. Definitely fingerpainted. And definitely turkeys.

That was enough proof that Hazel wasn't the Vandal.

But if she wasn't guilty then...

Okay, fine, she wasn't wrong. That was on me. I might've been a little aggressive earlier.

Anyways, we were cool after I apologized. She gave me the fist-bump of forgiveness before going back to the table with her friends.

Now that lunch was wrapping up, I headed toward the exit. Kids were starting to clear out. Trash cans were filling up. Tables were getting wiped down. And Davy Spencer was walking toward me with a fiery look in his eyes and... oh, come on...

Davy was pretty irked, demanding extra security to protect his potato. And even though I'M the one who almost hurt his potato, it suddenly occurred to me that Davy was right...

The Vandal was still on the loose, which meant the art show needed extra security if or when he'd try to strike again.

But something told me that it wasn't a matter of IF he'd strike again. It was a matter of WHEN.

Me and Vayla went out to patrol the halls between 5th and 6th period. I'm starting to really like our patrols together because it feels like we're starting to become buddy-buddies instead of just work-buddies...

We went around the school, but all was quiet, which was a good thing, obviously. So with nothing else to do, we went down to the cafeteria to check on our new art show monitors... Fergus and Dutch.

In case you don't know, Fergus and Dutch are only volunteer Hall Monitors, which means they get an orange sash, but can only use the power of the sash during lunch.

Davy asked them to do him a solid, and since they're all bros, they said yes. I mean, even though Fergus and Dutch were only part-timers, I was fine with it.

But only because they were better than Davy's FIRST choice...

Honestly, I kinda wanted to roll with it because I wanted to see if Chuck would actually stand around all day in medieval armor made out of pool noodles, but the other part of me wanted to actually protect the artwork on the stage.

But seriously, Sir Chuck of Metropolis??

Knight of Wobblybottom??

What?!?

After that, me and Vayla went over to check in on Espinoza and Lovejoy's sign. At that point, I'd kinda given up on those two ever wrapping their project up together because of how much they'd been bickering over it.

But when we got there, I was surprised to see them happily working with each other. They must've finally broken through whatever wall was between them.

79

Anyways – WHATEVER the reason – their sign was finally taking shape, and I gotta say – it was SUPES impressive.

They still had some work to do on it, but it was just little things left – a little paint here, a couple nails there.

I think their biggest obstacle for finishing it on time was figuring how to wire the whole thing so all the lightbulbs would flip on with one switch...

75 lightbulbs?? That was a whole lotta lightbulbs!

Apparently, their plan was for the sign to shine down on the winning artwork for the whole room to see.

Made sense. Sounded awesome. But 75 lightbulbs??

I mean, I wasn't sure how they were gonna pull that off, but I figured they had a plan...

So, with alls well at the school, me and Vayla headed out to the lobby to wait for 7th period to get out, and that's when we saw the weirdest things we'd ever seen in our lives...

The way I was supposed to contact Skullcap was to leave a balloon with his face on it, but I guess it worked the other way around, too.

I was pretty cool with it, but Vayla was a little creeped out, I guess...

I assumed Skullcap wanted to meet in the same bathroom on the second floor, so I ran up there while Vayla went on patrol alone.

Where'd he even get a balloon with my face on it?

Was that just something you can order on the internet? Because if it IS something I can order, I might get some for the whole squad.

I mean, just for fun.

Not as a form of communication.

Anyways, when I got upstairs, I found that Skullcap wasn't ONLY waiting for me in the bathroom. He'd been waiting a REALLY long time...

I had no idea who Skullcap was, but if he could get away with hanging out in the bathroom for AN HOUR AND A HALF and NOT getting in trouble for missing class, it could only mean one thing – he must've had study hall right after lunch.

Study hall teachers are just normal teachers who spend one period out of their day down in the study hall, and when they do, they're usually buried in work, grading papers.

Attendance doesn't always get taken, so... that was the only way Skullcap could get away with missing his whole 5th period.

If I wanted to learn his identity, I'd have to take a look at the 5th period study hall attendance list.

I was gonna have to remember to look into that later, but until then...

Skullcap handed me an 8x10 black and white photo of 32 kids grouped together – 17 of them standing, 15 of them kneeling in front, and all smiling at the camera.

It was the Walking Club.

And it was a little more popular than I thought.

I guess walking is the new cool.

I tried pinch zooming the shoes on the kids, but then remembered this was an actual photo – not a phone. So instead, I brought it up closer to my face, squinted hard, and suddenly realized...

Bro, EVERY SINGLE kid in this club is wearing Reebuks!

Uh, yeah, they get them when they join the club.

Perfect, just perfect!

32 on TOP of the 44 from the art show were too many suspects!

No, wait, 45 now that Davy was in the show, too.

That picture helped NOTHING.

I looked again, wondering if I could cross-reference or whatever the word was to figure out which kids from the Walking Club were also in the art show, but then I realized THAT was pointless since Mr. Reynolds STILL hadn't gotten me the list of kids in the show yet, and UGH!

Just UGH!!

And just when I was about to storm outta that bathroom in frustration, Skullcap goes...

I couldn't believe my earballs.

Skullcap had just said that the Vandal was CHARLOTTE, one of my Hall Monitors.

One of my best friends!

I wanted to argue – to say he was WRONG – but he even confirmed it himself – he saw her put her feet up during lunch – her Reebuks had the stars worn off of them.

How could she have ruined Annie's painting?

Had she always been a bad guy or had something happened recently that turned her bad?

Why was she even a Hall Monitor?!

My insides felt like they were caving in... how could CHARLOTTE LOVEJOY betray me like that??

Oh, man, I don't think I've ever been that close to having a total psychological breakdown. Even after I found out it WASN'T Lovejoy, I had to take a second. Collect myself. Reset and splash some cold water on my face.

I grabbed a paper towel and wiped my face, turning back to Skullcap to get more deets about Shawcross, but by then, he was already gone...

No matter. I had what I needed. Shawcross was next on the list to question about Annie's painting.

All I needed to do was match her shoe to the footprint I had taken a picture of, and that was it – case closed.

Or, at least, I HOPED that was it...

Just before school got out, me and Vayla went down to the art room to pay good ol' Mr. Reynolds a visit. He'd had ALL DAY to find the list of kids in the art show, so he HAD to have found it by now, right?

I mean, I can't blame him for taking so long. It's not like he's an actual teacher at the school – he's just a substitute.

Not that a sub ISN'T an actual teacher – that's not what I meant – just that subs don't really have their own space at the schools they sub at. They're kinda just thrown into a room and left to the wolves.

Anyways, we went to the art room, but Mr. Reynolds wasn't around when we got there. The room was empty, and the lights were off...

No answer.

I wanted to go inside and rummage around to find the list of kids on my own, but I didn't have a warrant.

Honestly, I don't know for sure what a "warrant" even is. All I know is that cops get in trouble when they do stuff without one, so that was enough to keep me from entering the room. I'd almost lost the Hall Monitor program last season, and I wasn't about to risk losing it again.

But not Vayla.

She didn't care.

So I let Vayla do her thing as I walked around the empty halls, but it turns out that I hadn't totally missed Mr. Reynolds. He was outside, on his way to the parking lot.

That's when the last bell jangled, and students began pouring out of classrooms. Shouts of victory bounced off metal lockers from kids done with the daily grind.

They were free. Untethered. Wild.

The end of school is always the most hectic part of the day for a Hall Monitor – I was needed.

But I also needed to ask Mr. Reynolds about that list!

I mean, Vayla was back in the art room looking for it, but if she came up empty, then we'd need Mr. Reynolds to help us anyway, so...

I pushed the door open and sprinting, but alas – I wasn't fast enough.

I got to the end of the sidewalk just in time to watch the substitute art teacher drive off in his shiny convertible...

I was bummed.

But I gotta admit that I was actually more interested in the fact that he was driving a one of those new Cobra Spitfires.

I'm not a "car guy," but even I know those things are pretty baller.

Anyways, running outside wasn't a total waste of time because that's when I spotted Charlotte Shawcross making her way to the bus lines. So I switched gears and started jogging in her direction, but it didn't take long for me to get cut off by a couple kids whose only purpose in life is to give me a hard time...

Evie and Elijah Lee.

Sister and brother.

Student Patrol.

Those two are like the candy corn of people.

Look, I don't know when the feud started between Hall Monitors and Student Patrols, but it's been there for as long as I can remember.

Some say it even goes back to the late 1800's around the time when public schools were first created.

Apparently, some wad from the original Hall Monitor program got booted for being too harsh, so he left and started his own program instead, which we now call Student Patrol.

I had my doubts about the story, but Fergus showed me a picture of them...

Anyways, for some reason, Evie and Elijah think that being OUTSIDE is way more important than being INSIDE.

It's like they think there's some kind of competition between Student Patrol and Hall Monitors or something when CLEARLY there isn't because the Hall Monitors are just better in every way.

I tried slipping past those two, but they kept darting back and forth, blocking my path.

The line for Shawcross' bus had started moving forward. If I couldn't get to her in the next minute, then I was gonna have to wait until the morning.

And I HATE waiting until the morning.

So instead of trying to dodge Evie and Elijah, I tried reasoning with them. As evil as those two were, they were still good kids – they'd understand.

I explained to them the exact situation – that I wasn't trying to step on their toes, and that I was only outside to question Charlotte about Annie's destroyed painting.

And you know what? They totally understood.

But then – as I should've known – Evie totally spun around and zoomed off to get to Shawcross before I could...

Evie was fast – no surprise there – since she is, in fact, the star runner on Wood's 8th grade track team. She ran like a 5 minute, 15 second mile which makes her the fastest 8th grader in the state and, like, sixth fastest in the whole freakin' country.

So yeah.

There was no way I was gonna catch her.

But I wasn't about to go out like a punk, so I ran as hard as my short, little 6th grade legs could go, every muscle in my body blazing, but it still wasn't even CLOSE to fast enough.

Evie sailed across the sidewalk like she was Barry Allen, AKA, the Flash – or Ivana Molotova, AKA, LADY Flash for all the comic book fans out there.

But just when Evie was about to win the race to Shawcross, some rando on a skateboard swerved in front of her.

Wood Intermediate has ZERO tolerance when it comes to skating on school property thanks to countless broken bones over the years.

PRINCIPAL HAWKINS

Evie slid to a stop.

She looked at Shawcross.

Then back at me.

Then at the kid on the skateboard.

Then back to Shawcross.

Evie's brain was calculating, trying to decide whether to go after Shawcross or to go after the kid on the board.

Going after Shawcross was a risk – she might not be guilty but going after the skater was a surefire bust.

Lucky for me, I didn't care about the skater, which was the only reason I was able to dash past Evie.

I heard Evie's frustrated groan as she turned on her heel to pursue the skater instead.

With Evie out of the race, I slowed to catch my breath, clutch at the cramp in my side, and try my best not to barf in front of everybody there.

I'd never run that hard in my life, and I was definitely feelin' it. But I kept pushing myself to get to Shawcross, and I'm proud to say that I was able to reach her before she boarded her bus...

Yup.

Shawcross was wearing Reebuks.

And they were definitely missing their stars.

I got up and laid it all out for her – Annie's destroyed painting, the water underneath it, the footprints, her shoes, the missing stars – all were connected and all pointed back at her...

YOU ruined Annie's painting! YOU threw the water balloon! YOU are the Vandal! I have BUSTED you, and you are now BUSTED!!

At last, the case was solved.

I stood there proudly, basking in my victory... there was a lot less cheering than I thought there would be.

I mean, it wasn't like there was NO cheering.

There was just less of it than I'd imagined.

But my victory didn't last long because after all the cheering settled down, Shawcross goes...

EPISODE FOURTEEN:
TURTLE ASSISTANCE
THURSDAY, 3:10 p.m.

Me and Lovejoy ran out of the gym doors and all the way down to the football field that the track wrapped around to find and move the turtle that Gymalski had called about.

She never said where exactly it was, so me and Lovejoy had to jog around the whole thing to search for it, but by then, the turtle was long gone.

Sometimes calls like that work themselves out... but not this time.

On our way back to the school, Lovejoy spotted the turtle of interest, but he wasn't on the track. He was in the MIDDLE OF THE STREET next to the track, with cars passing by him and everything.

Lovejoy took the lead, running out to the street to help the poor little guy cross without getting hurt...

I probably shoulda asked Charlotte a few questions yesterday before straight-up accusing her in front of everybody, but I KINDA figured Skullcap had already done that.

I mean, he SHOULD have!

If that dude wanted to be like Batman, then he was gonna have to step up his detective game, like, for realskies.

Anyways, as soon as I got to school, I headed to HQ, surprised to see that Vayla was already there.

Part of me just wanted to give up on the whole case.

I mean, nobody else seemed to care about finding the Vandal - not even ANNIE - so why should we?

I took the thick stack of papers anyway because I knew it was the right thing to do. And when I say the stack was "thick" I mean "THICK."

The thing was like a NOVEL with TONS of pages all held together by one fat clip on the top corner.

It wasn't just a list of names that Vayla had found.

No, it was a copy of the grant document that Mr. Reynolds had used to get money from the city.

On the front page there was even a small red stamp that said, "FUNDING APPROVED."

I flipped through the first few pages - official blah

blah blah junk that I didn't understand – until I finally found the list of names I'd been looking for.

With 45 kids in the art show, you'd think that a single page would cover it, but apparently not. Apparently, the grant document had to make it one of the most confusing lists in the world by including EVERY SINGLE 6th grader at Wood on it, which looked to be about 200 total according to that document.

I mean, ME and VAYLA's names were on the list, and I knew WE weren't IN the art show.

She was right.

It WAS weird.

Vayla took her phone out and snapped photos of the pages with all the names. She wanted to look into some of the names on her own time, I guess.

And I would've kept flipping through the pages, but

that's when Mr. Reynolds showed up at our door.

Mr. Reynolds took the document, confused. He sifted through the pages, brow furrowed, studying the random names. Suddenly, his face perked up, and he nodded like a lightbulb had switched on in his dome...

Mr. Reynolds bounced, after that, and I didn't go after him.

I mean, I wanted to ask what the extra names were all about, but by then, I was just done with the roller coaster of emotions. Every single lead I followed had been an absolute flop.

That list of names was the last thing that gave me ANY kind of hope, but that, too, was now gone with the freakin' wind.

I was gonna have to face facts – the kid who splashed Annie's painting was gonna get away with it.

And there was not a thing I could do about it.

The rest of the morning was pretty boring, nothing fun to report. And I don't mean "fun" like a circus clown or anything – I mean "fun" like I-finally-found-the-Vandal-and-was-given-the-key-to-the-city fun.

Although circus clowns DO have a way of making the parts of our lives that have gone stale fun again, like that time I hired one for Principal Hawkins' birthday...

Anyways, there was still half a school day left until the art show during 8th period. That's when ALL the 6th graders were gonna be allowed out of their classes to come and chill in the cafeteria with snacks and juice boxes and music and stuff.

That's also when Mr. Reynolds was gonna announce the winner of the show and hand them the brand spankin' new ArtPad Pro, which definitely WOULDN'T BE Annie now that she was out of the contest.

And just so you know – Davy was still in the lead, but Josh Lucey's octophant was catching up pretty fast.

So, right before lunch started, me and Vayla went and visited Espinoza and Lovejoy one last time to check on their "Winner!" sign.

Aside from a few missing lightbulbs, they were pretty much done with it.

And I gotta say – it looked AMAZEBALLS.

At least... I THINK it did.

When all the lights on that thing were turned on, it was actually kinda hard to see anything at all...

I don't know where those two found 75 lightbulbs, but I knew better than to ask. All I told them was that the lightbulbs needed to be put back where they came from IMMEDIATELY after the show.

I just hoped the lights weren't taken from anywhere important...

The four of us rolled that bad boy to the cafeteria as our mobile unit escorted us...

Students in their classrooms pointed at us all excited as we passed their doorways. I was SUPER proud of the work that Espinoza and Lovejoy had done and was happy that they were gettin' mad props for it.

When lunch started, Principal Hawkins and Mr. Reynolds helped put the sign up on the stage, and there it stood for everybody to admire in all its glory.

Too bad the sign was only up there for about 30 seconds before Davy tried moving his spud under it. Oh, and BTW, his potato was now starting to rot...

EPISODE SEVENTEEN:
URGENT PACKAGE DELIVERY
FRIDAY, 11:15 a.m.

Lovejoy and Vayla got an emergency call straight from Principal Hawkins about a VIP package that had gotten delivered to the wrong side of the school, so the two of them immediately dispatched to the location of the misdelivered package.

After securing it, they bolted through a sea of students, carefully keeping the contents of the package safe in Lovejoy's hands...

Finally, after a record-breaking race from one end of the school to the other, Lovejoy and Vayla made it to the front office, successfully delivering the package to Hawkins himself, who then proceeded to open it in front of them and reveal what was inside...

The 8th period bell had just finished ringing, which meant that the art show had officially begun. Every 6th grader at Wood had been told to come directly to the cafeteria instead of going to their classes.

The stage was packed. Pretty much every 6th grader at the school – all 200 of them apparently – was up there, scoping all the cool artwork.

Mr. Reynolds had also done a great job dressing up the place. Tons of big balloons and ribbons. Apple and fruit punch juice boxes. A whole buffet of delicious brownies, cookies, and kinda gross cheese danishes.

I'm sorry, I'm just not a fan of danishes.

It was honestly pretty cool even though all of it was only possible cuz the city gave Mr. Reynolds the money to do it.

So all of that together made the place feel less like a cafeteria and more like an art gallery, which also made a couple of kids forget they were only 6th graders and NOT art snobs from a big city...

My Hall Monitors kept a keen eye on things, especially because we all knew the Vandal was still out there. Even though I wasn't on the case anymore didn't mean I was gonna put my guard down.

No way. At any moment, he could strike again.

Vayla was by my side. Espinoza and Lovejoy were stationed at the foot of the stage. Chad was by the exits, one foot on the ground and the other on his scooter.

And Fergus and Dutch were by Davy's potato again, but in a surprise twist, Davy's potato had lost the lead to Josh Lucey's drawing of an octophant.

Obviously, Davy wasn't too happy about that, but he wasn't about to give up.

He thought touching up his potato might pull in the extra votes needed to win, so he asked if he could run to his locker and grab his paint marker.

Last second touch ups weren't against the rules, but Davy alone in the hallways is NEVER a good idea, so I just told him that I'd go get it for him instead, which he was cool with, so he gave me his locker combination.

Since grabbing a paint marker wasn't a two-man job, I went by myself. With Vayla, Chad, Espinoza, and Lovejoy in the cafeteria, I wasn't too worried about the show.

I mean, by that point, the school day was almost over. There was, like, 20 minutes left until the end of the day, and Mr. Reynolds was probably gonna start counting tokens pretty soon. If the Vandal hadn't struck again by now, then he probably wasn't gonna strike at all.

I was even beginning to think that maybe the Vandal WASN'T someone in the show who wanted to win the ArtPad Pro. Maybe it was just some random jerk who wanted to destroy something beautiful, y'know?

I got to Davy's locker, and in the stillness of the hallway, I spun his numbers on the dial...

Then I pulled up on the handle, swung the door open, and looked inside. To my surprise, it wasn't as messy as I thought it was gonna be. Here I expected a locker packed tight with garbage and moldy food, but it wasn't like that at all.

In fact, it was pretty organized.

A few comics at the bottom. Two unopened cans of Squinty Soda™. One bag of spicy chips. An opened package of water balloons.

My gaze moved steadily up the metal cabinet, looking for the paint marker that Davy had asked for.

On the hanger were two hoodies. Behind those was a mirror stuck to the back wall.

Still no paint marker.

So I searched higher, raising myself on my tippy-toes, peeking at the top shelf.

And that's when I suddenly stopped. An electric shock zipped through my body as my eyes locked in place.

At the top of Davy's locker was a blue paint marker.

Sitting right next to a pair of purple-splattered Reebuks...

I couldn't believe it.

I couldn't FREAKING believe it.

The shoes that I'd been looking for all week had been hidden in Davy Spencer's locker the whole time!! Not only were they missing the stars on the heels, but they were splattered with purple paint!

THOSE shoes were the ones that had made the footprints in the cafeteria!

DAVY SPENCER had destroyed Annie's painting!

WHAT THE WHAT?!?

I continued staring – no, GAWKING – at the evidence while my brain connected the dots...

Davy was in the cafeteria on Thursday morning, but he came in immediately AFTER the suspect had left.

He wasn't wearing the Reebuks, but he could've easily changed shoes in the hallway and come right back inside so he wouldn't look suspicious!

His locker even had an open package of water balloons in it! Man, the evidence was piling up!

The painting that he ruined was an embarrassing one of HIM. And now that Annie was out of the contest, HE was gonna win the ArtPad Pro!

That's when it suddenly hit me...

If Davy had destroyed Annie's painting, then he was gonna do it again to Josh's drawing, for sure!

I looked at the time – only 15 minutes until the end of the day. Mr. Reynolds was gonna start counting tokens at any second.

I only had seconds to stop the Vandal – DAVY SPENCER – from striking again.

So I grabbed the Reebuks and started tearing through the halls to get back to the cafeteria before it was too late.

The cafeteria was clear across the building, but with how hard I was running it only took a few seconds to get there. When I pulled the door open, I was rekt...

Mr. Reynolds hadn't started counting tokens yet, thankfully, but he was about to. I wanted to shout at him, but my throat was dry and catching my voice, so it just came out as weird caveman grunts...

That's when I saw Davy making his move, moseying on over to Josh's octophant. I had to get up there IMMEDIATELY, but my legs were like strawberry Jell-O.

So I grabbed Chad's scooter and blasted off.

Principal Hawkins wasn't gonna be happy about it, but he'd understand after I stopped Davy from committing a crime against the art world.

I flew across that lunchroom like I was on the wings of an eagle, finally finding my voice and shouting at Mr. Reynolds to stop the show.

Everybody stopped and turned to look at the kid streaming across the room on a scooter.

I wasn't sure how fast that thing could go, but I was definitely going faster than I intended.

My fingers reached for the brake handle to skid to a stop, but that's when I realized Chad's scooter didn't have brakes.

So instead of scraping a cool half-circle on the floor, I hit the side of the stage at max speed and flew off that thing like a rag doll superman.

My body sailed about a foot above the wooden planks, passing students and teachers until I finally smashed into one of the pedestals, taking it – and the piece of art on top of it – out completely.

A crowd gathered around me. Mr. Reynolds ran over to make sure I was alright. I rolled to my back and suddenly felt some kind of mush underneath me, like I had rolled on top of a nubble of Play-Doh.

A horrid smell suddenly filled my nose holes as I reached back, grabbing the soft blob. I brought it around to look at it, and realized that it wasn't Play-Doh that I had smooshed up – it was actually...

The crowd gathered around me, kinda speechless. I say "kinda" because even though it was quiet, there were still some hushed whispers floating around.

Mr. Reynolds and Principal Hawkins pushed through

the crowd. Hawkins was ready to blow up at me, I could tell. He was mad, obvi, but I knew that he'd understand after I explained everything – that Davy was about to wreck Josh's art and I had all the evidence to prove he had wrecked Annie's, so I hopped to my feet and started spilling the tea...

The crowd gasped. I gasped. Davy and Mr. Reynolds gasped. Every single person in the cafeteria gasped.

Except for one – Annie.

She was cool as a cucumber, watching everything with a little smirk on her face, almost like the whole thing was funny to her, which was a little unnerving, if you asked me, but everybody deals with grief in their own way, right?

No big deal.

I solved the case.

Sure, it was a small case, but it was still a case!

I worked my buns off through blood, sweat, and tears! Well, not blood, but sweat and tears, for sure!

Anyways, my point is that a case is a case, and the Case of the Sabotaged Painting had officially been cracked.

Or... at least, I thought it had.

Right up until Annie said...

Those are MY shoes. I put them in Davy's locker after they got all wet on Thursday morning. We share lockers, remember?

Okay, hold up.

Annie just said the Reebuks belonged to HER even though I'd found them in Davy's locker, and that she had changed out of them because they got all wet on Thursday morning...

Okay, but... why were they wet?

Because of the water balloon I popped. Got that from Davy's locker, too.

Wait, wait, wait...

My brain. It was starting to hurt, but can you blame it?? It was burning 1,000 calories a second trying to wrap my head around the situation!

So - let me get this straight - ANNIE'S Reebuks had gotten wet on Thursday morning from one of Davy's water balloons that she HERSELF had popped.

After that, she went to Davy's locker, changed out of the shoes, leaving them there to dry, and...

Ugh! No matter how many ways I tried looking at it, I just couldn't understand!

What was Annie saying??

I couldn't believe it. The Case of the Sabotaged Painting was a lie! The hard work that we'd spent running around and investigating was all for nothing!

That's when a flood of different emotions came rushing in on me – anger, shame, humiliation, embarrassment, annoyance, regret – so fast that I couldn't help myself, and right there onstage in front of all 200 6th graders – I lost it.

Was Principal Hawkins that out of touch with his own school that he didn't know how many 6th graders went there? Mr. Reynold's grant document CLEARLY had 200 in it – me and Vayla had even counted them.

But when I started to explain that to Hawkins, Mr. Reynolds was quick to interrupt...

I even volunteered to get the copy of the grant document from the art room, but Mr. Reynolds said that he had already shredded it.

I don't know, maybe it was just me, but that seemed a little sus and pretty irresponsible.

But it wasn't that big of a deal because that's when Vayla pulled her phone out...

Everything happened so fast after that. Nobody really knew what the heck was going on. Something about Vayla's picture of the grant document freaked Mr. Reynolds out, and he made a mad dash for the door.

But he didn't get far.

Davy's stanktastic mashed potato was still on the floor, and when Mr. Reynold's foot hit it, he slid across the stage like some kind of cartoon character until he flopped on his face, perfectly placed under Espinoza and Lovejoy's sign, which mysteriously switched on – all 75 lights burning brightly over the substitute art teacher.

And instead of trying to run again, Mr. Reynolds just laid there in pain, defeated...

Remember when I said I wished the Hall Monitors could just solve one big case?

Well, guess what? We totally did!

Okay, so peep this – the city gives schools who hold an art show $50 per student in the show to pay for prizes and food and drinks and stuff.

Our school has 50 6th graders in it – just like Hawkins had said – but only 45 of them entered the show, which means that the city should've given Mr. Reynolds only $2,250.

But since he wrote down TWO HUNDRED names, the city gave him TEN GRAND. So he set aside $2,250 for the school, and then pocketed the rest of that sweet cash for himself.

Not only THAT, but it turns out the dude's been doing that SAME THING at DIFFERENT schools for MONTHS!

And for those of you who want the Explain-Like-I'm-Five version – Mr. Reynolds had been stealing money from the city for a really long time.

Like, lots of money.

Enough to be rich.

I don't know if Mr. Reynolds got arrested or is under investigation or whatever, but I DO know that he's in a heck of a lot of trouble because the Hall Monitors totally caught the bad guy and saved the day!

Fine. Davy Spencer might've helped a little, too, but as far as Skullcap?

Anyways, after all that, the art show went on like normal. Ms. Bane even came back from her vacation early and decided to stop by the show before going home...

And FYI – Josh Lucey won the whole show, which meant he SHOULD'VE gotten the ArtPad Pro, but I guess that had to be confiscated as evidence or something.

No big deal, though, cuz Hawkins found something else to give Josh instead...

And – just so you know – it's not like we do this for the recognition, but the city DID give the Wood Hall Monitors a Courage Award to give us props for catching a legit criminal.

So... that was pretty nice.

And when the award came in the mail, Principal Hawkins asked us to pose with it for a yearbook photo. He was seriously proud of us and wanted to put the whole story in that year's edition, for sure.

So I got the squad together and lined us all up under Espinoza and Lovejoy's sign, but not before adding one extra letter to it.

Man, I love my squad so much.

That's it for this season of Hall Monitors, but before I peace out, I wanna say that I need your help figuring out what kind of awesome craziness is going to happen in the next season of Hall Monitors!

Decide what happens in the next HALL MONITORS book!

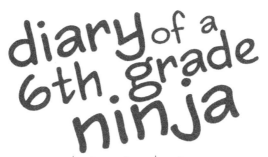

short comic adventure

BY MARCUS EMERSON

Marcus Emerson is the author and illustrator of a whole lot of books including the way popular DIARY OF A 6TH GRADE NINJA series, the KID YOUTUBER series, THE SUPER LIFE OF BEN BRAVER series, and the SECRET AGENT 6th GRADER series. His goal is to ~~make money~~ create children's books that are funny and inspirational for kids of all ages – even the adults who never grew up.

Marcus still dreams of becoming an astronaut and WALKING ON THE SUN, LIKE WHAT?? THAT'S NOT EVEN POSSIBLE.

Made in the USA
Las Vegas, NV
08 December 2024